DRAGONS

A Fantasy Coloring Book

by Jennifer Broschinsky

A Word from the Artist

Welcome, and I hope you enjoy this journey with my favorite mythical beasts! I love creating pen and ink drawings, and dragons have been one of my favorite subjects to draw since I was six. They've inspired my imagination in so many ways.

Like what you see? Consider subscribing to my Patreon! For $1 a month, you get a PDF download of a coloring page to print and color as often as you like!

Dragons: A Fantasy Coloring Book

Copyright © 2017 by Jennifer Broschinsky

Printed by CreateSpace, an Amazon.com company

Published by Jennifer Broschinsky, Puffbird Studio
www.puffbird.net
www.patreon.com/puffbird

ISBN: 978-1979973779

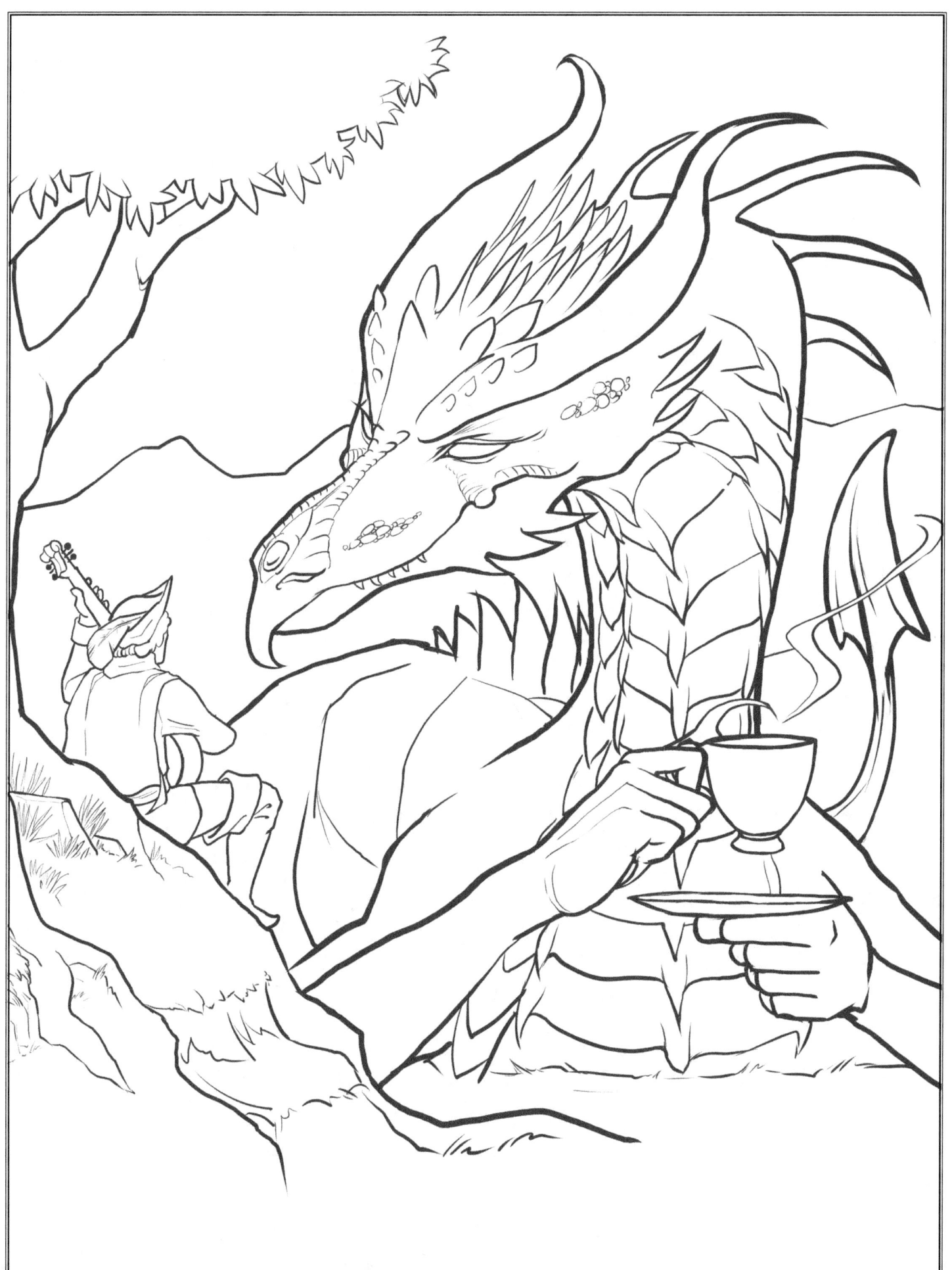

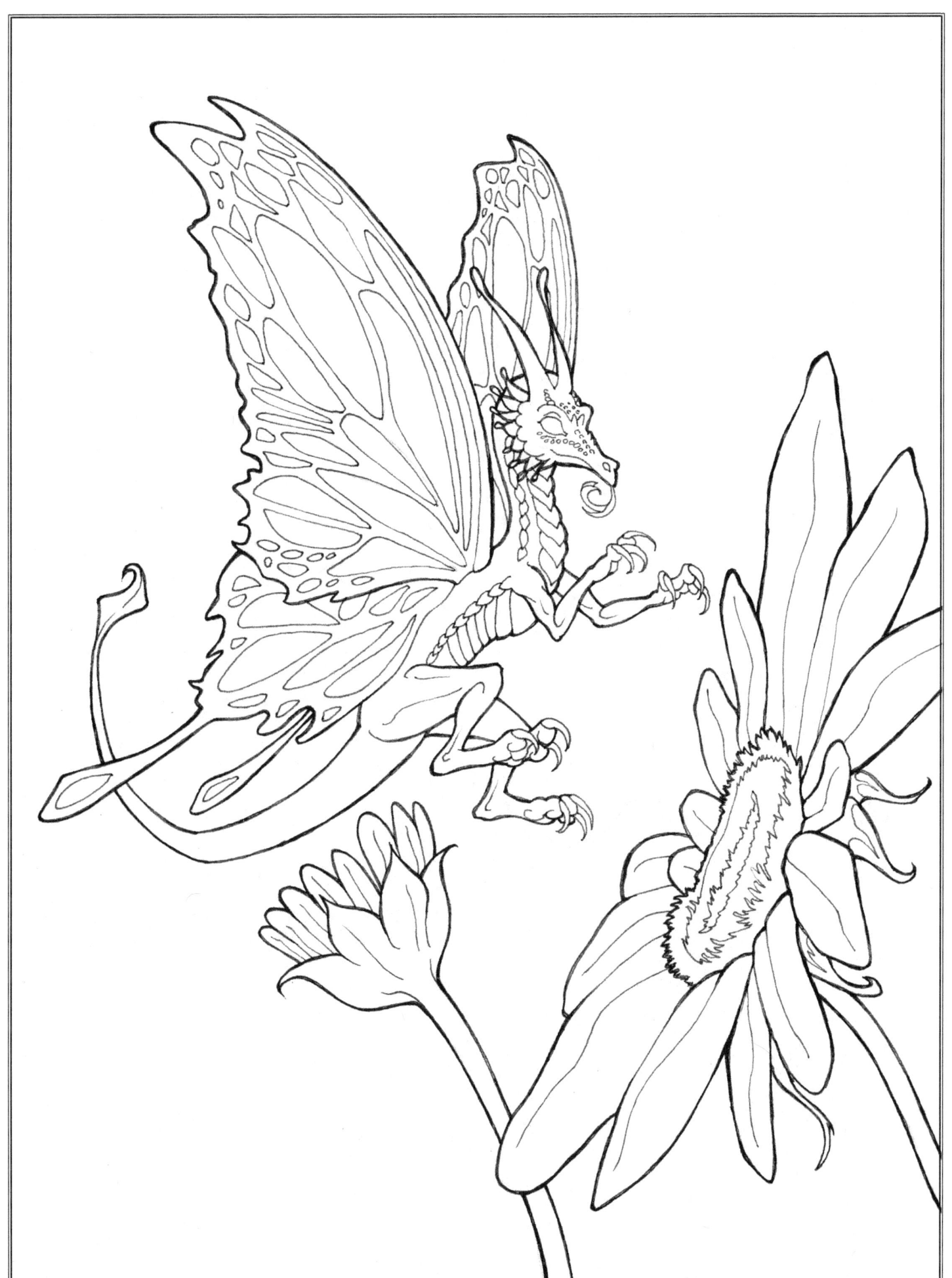

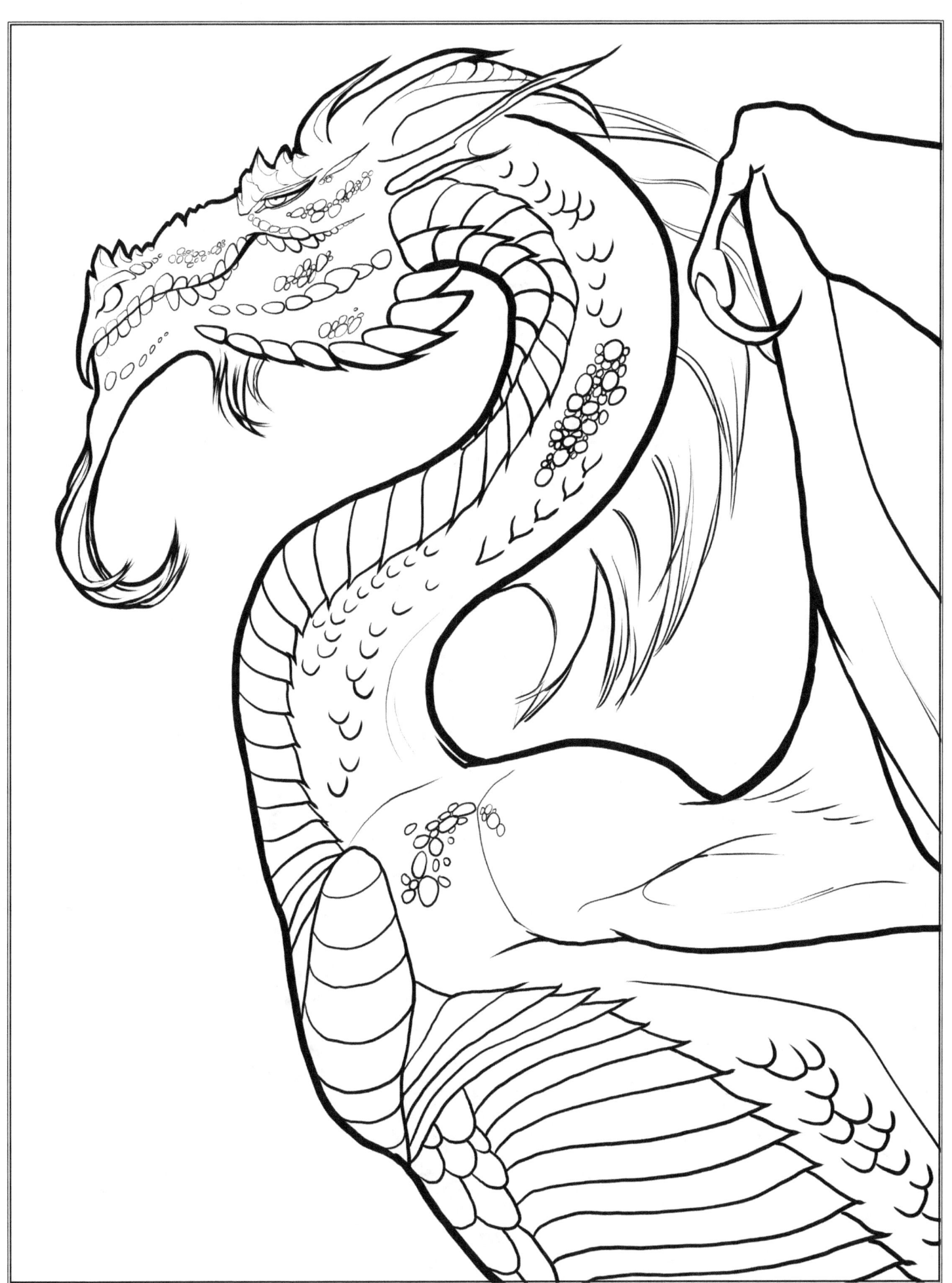

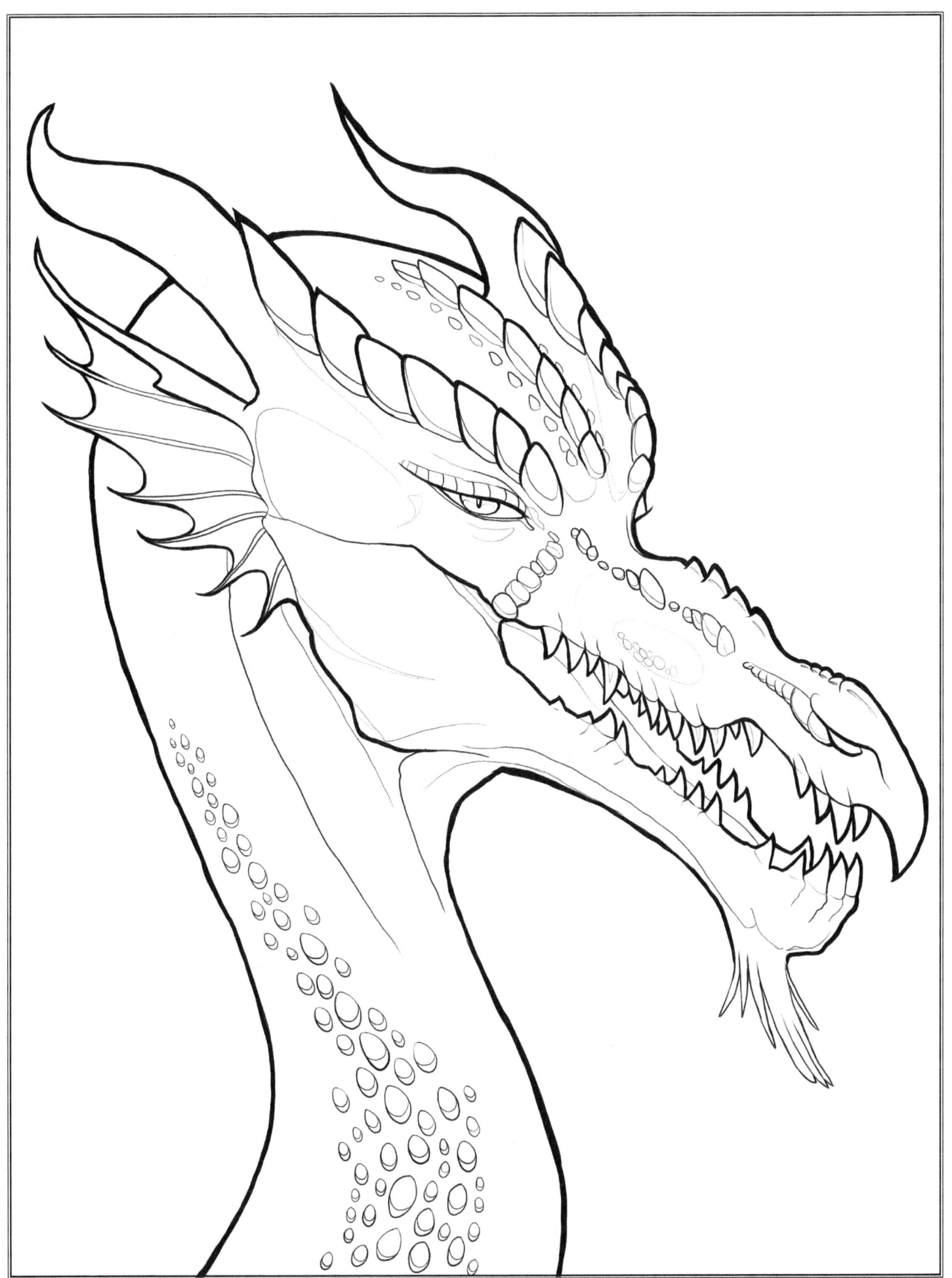

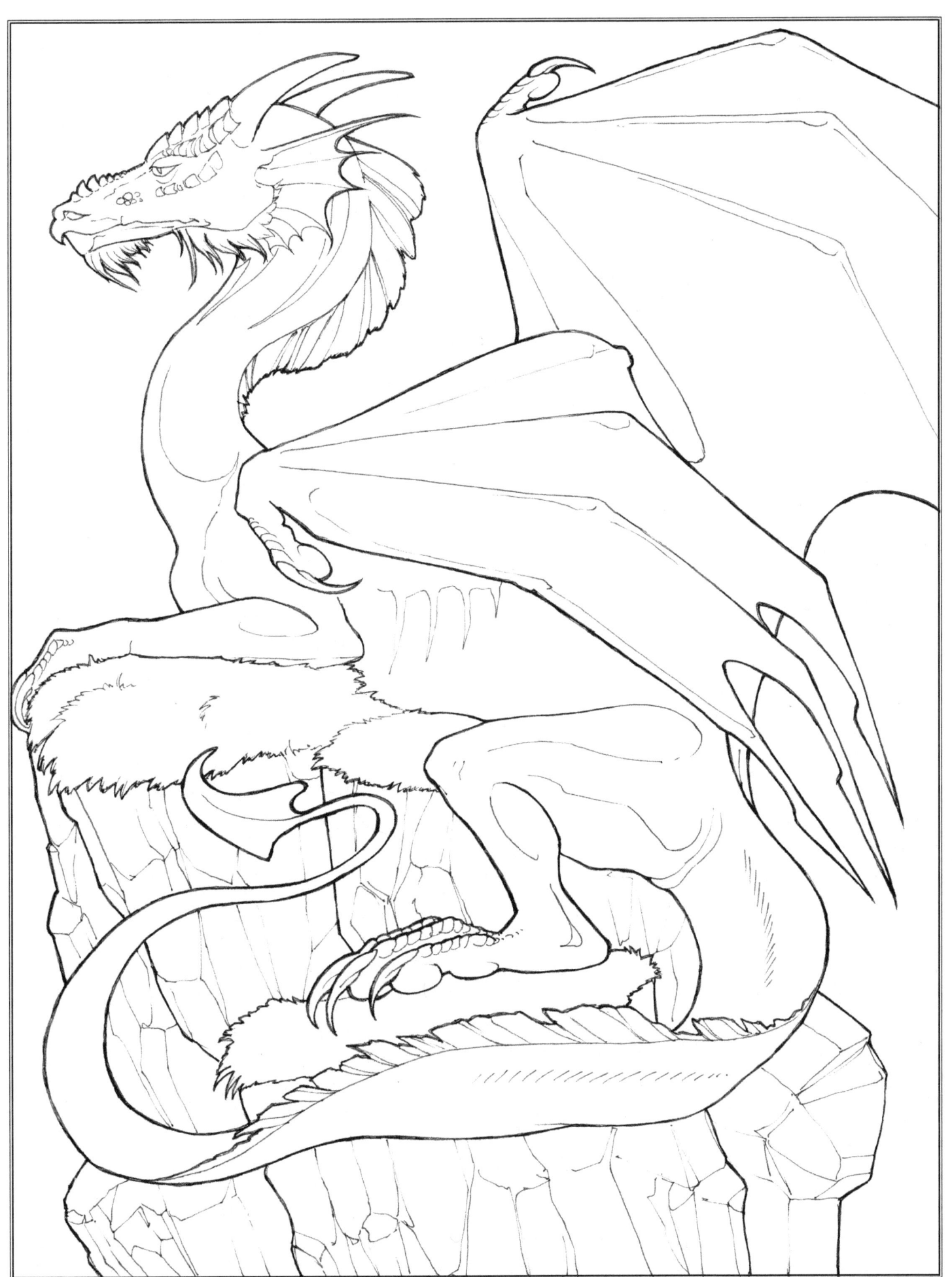

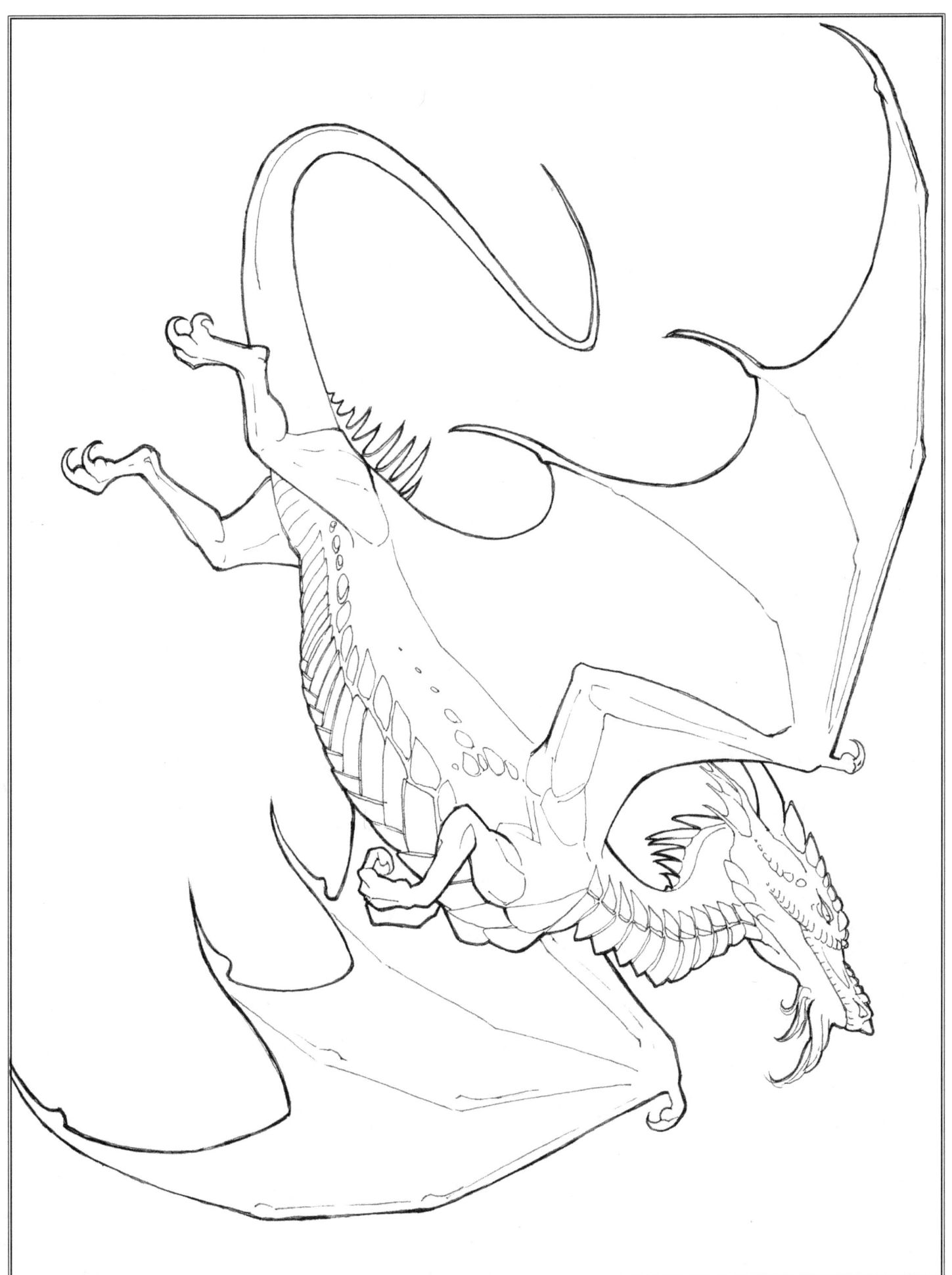

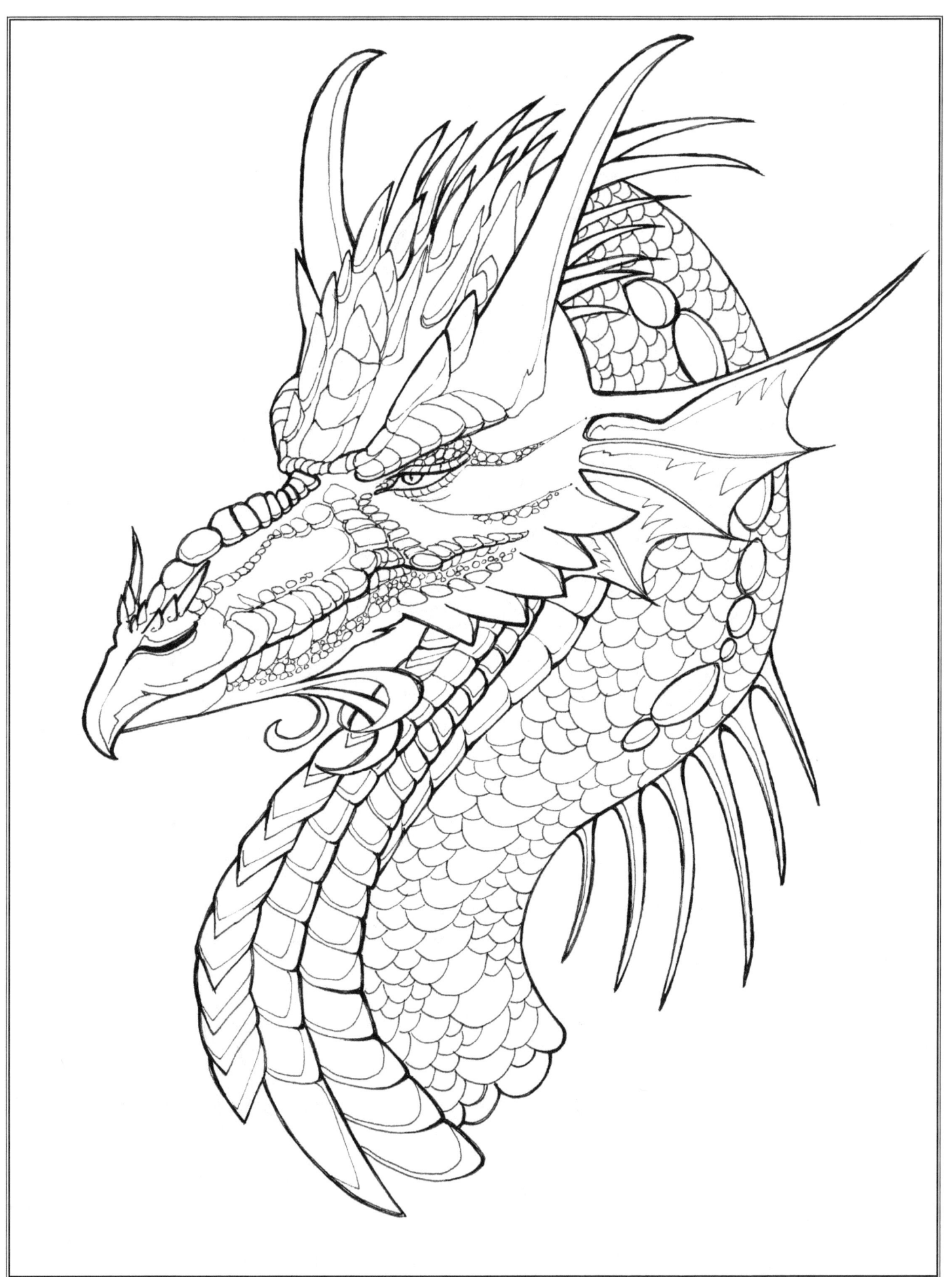

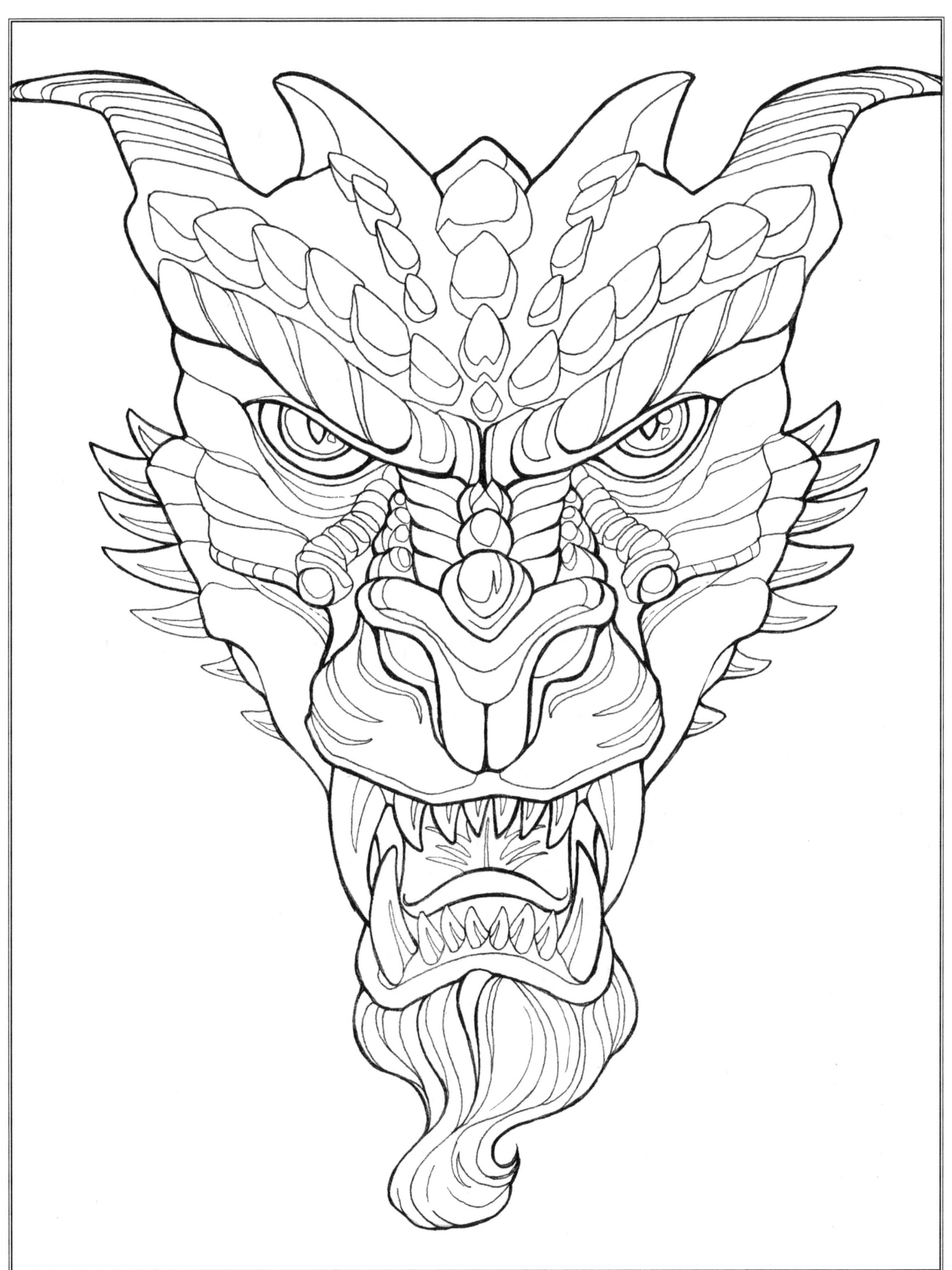

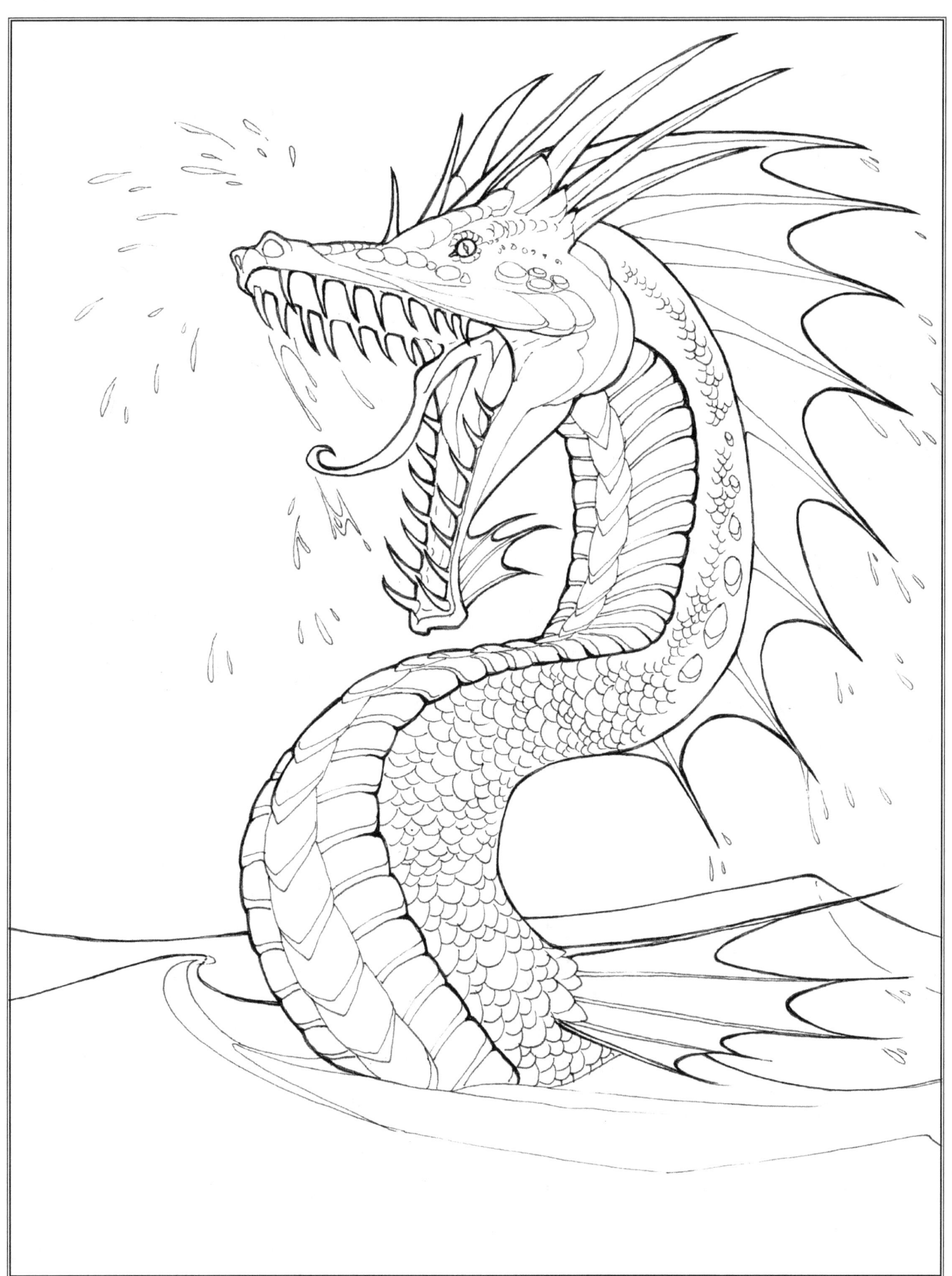

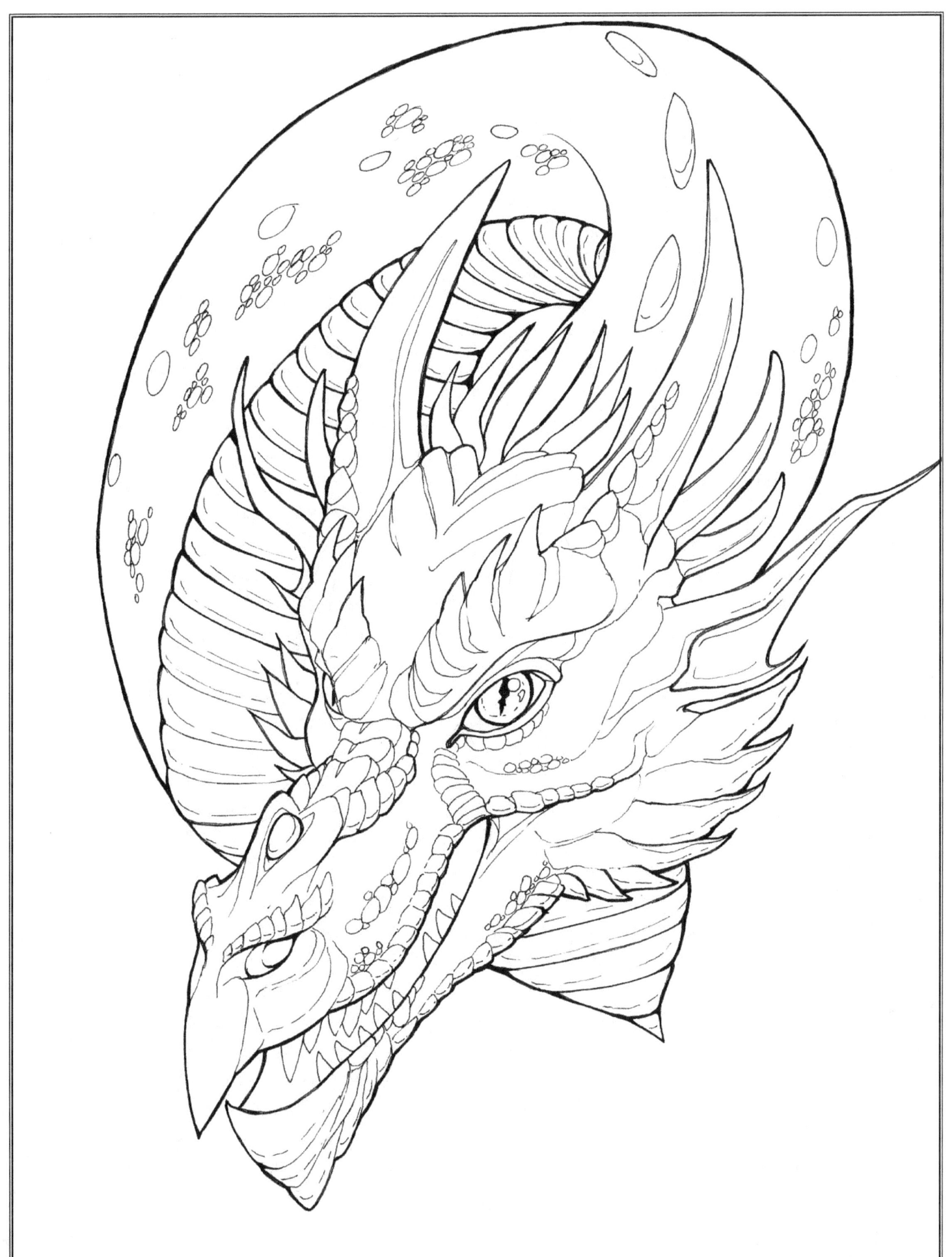

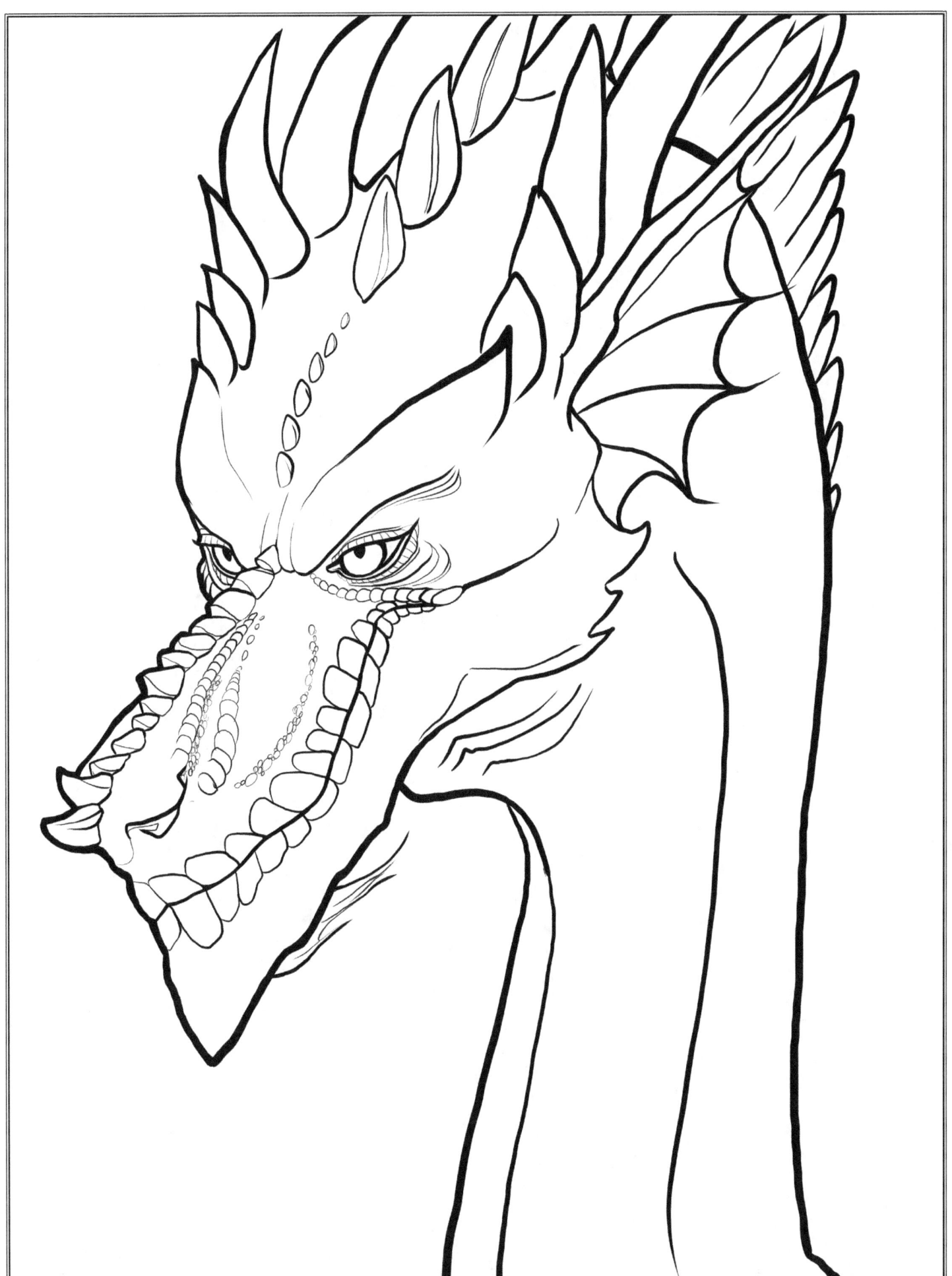

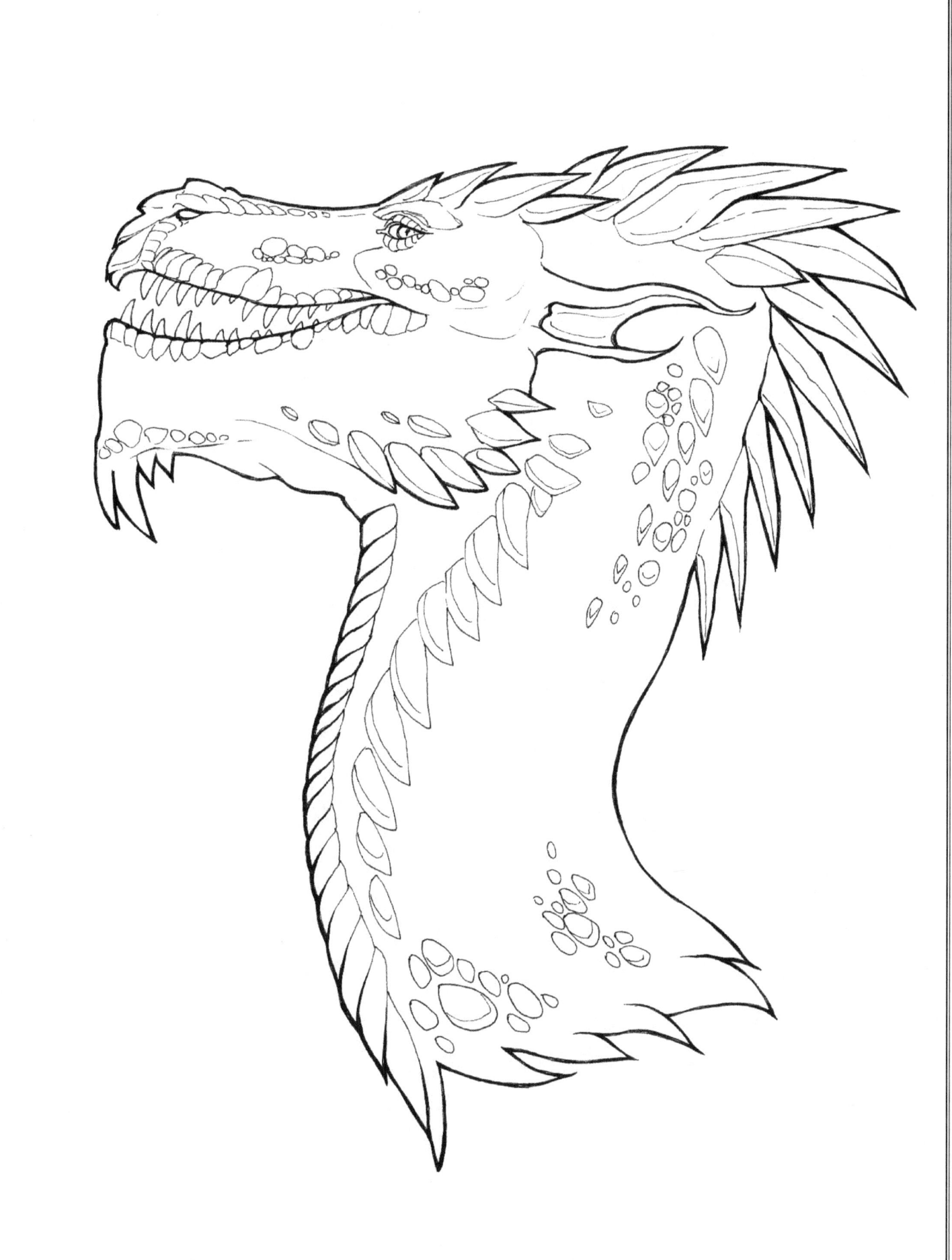

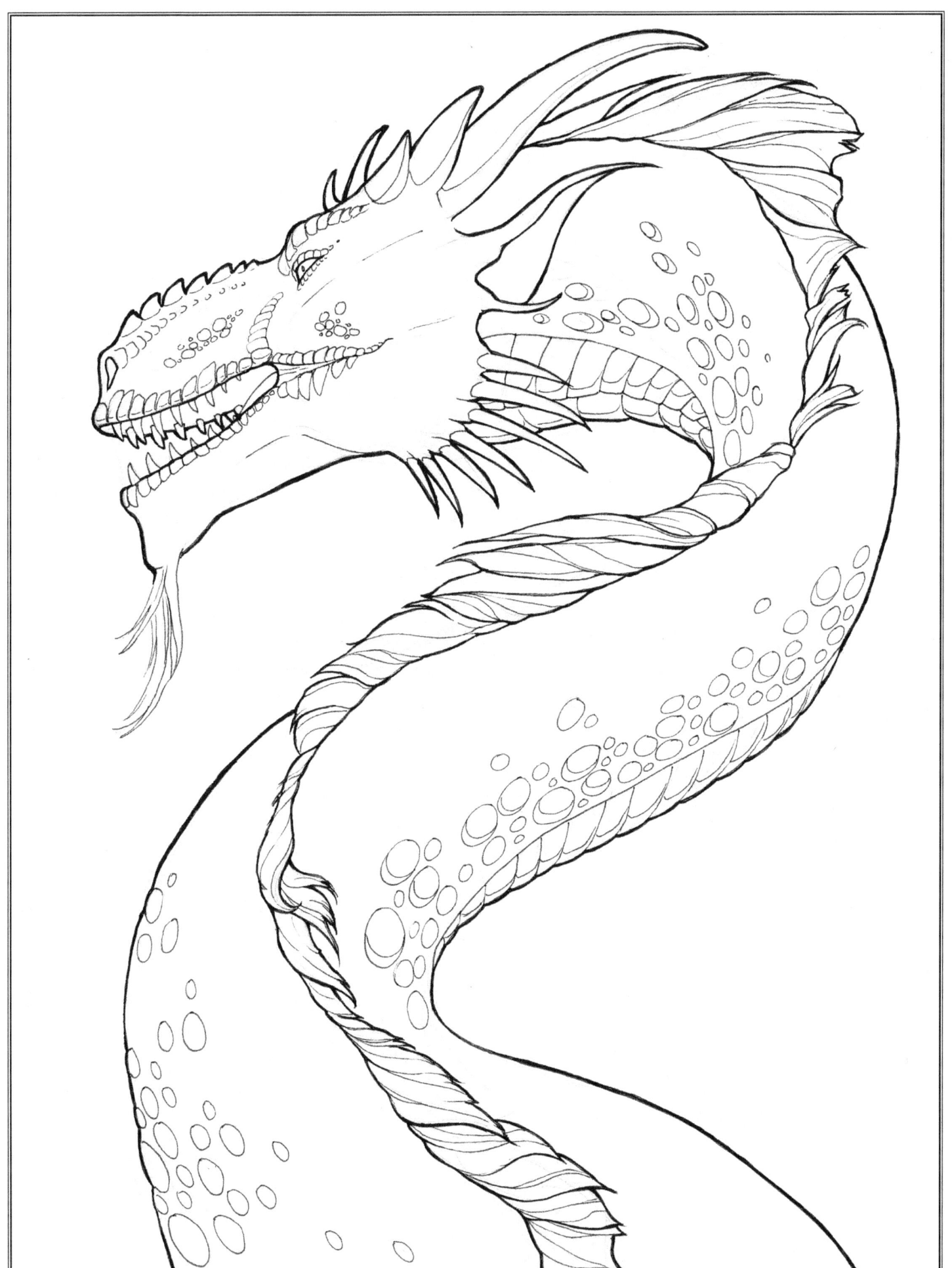

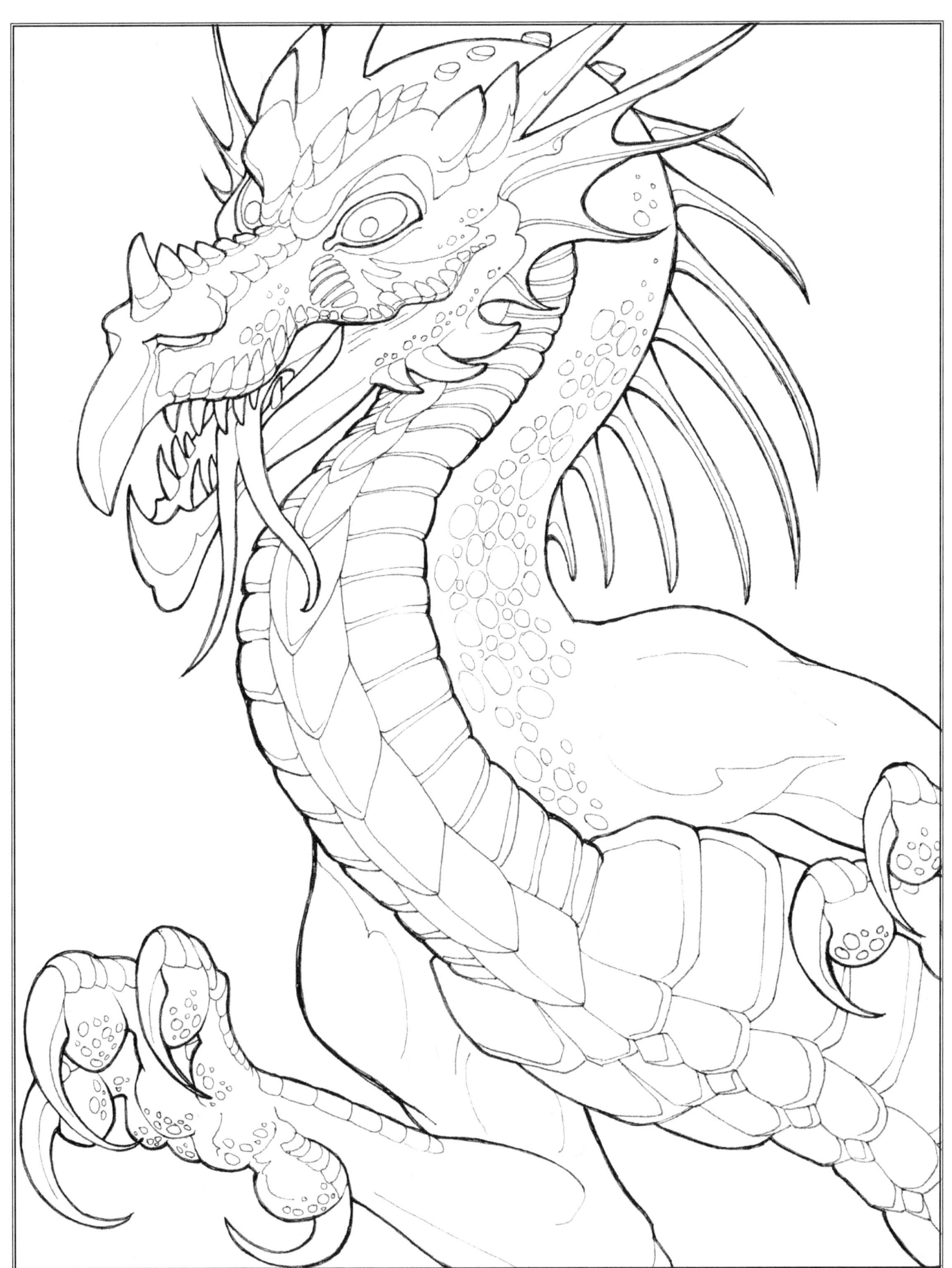

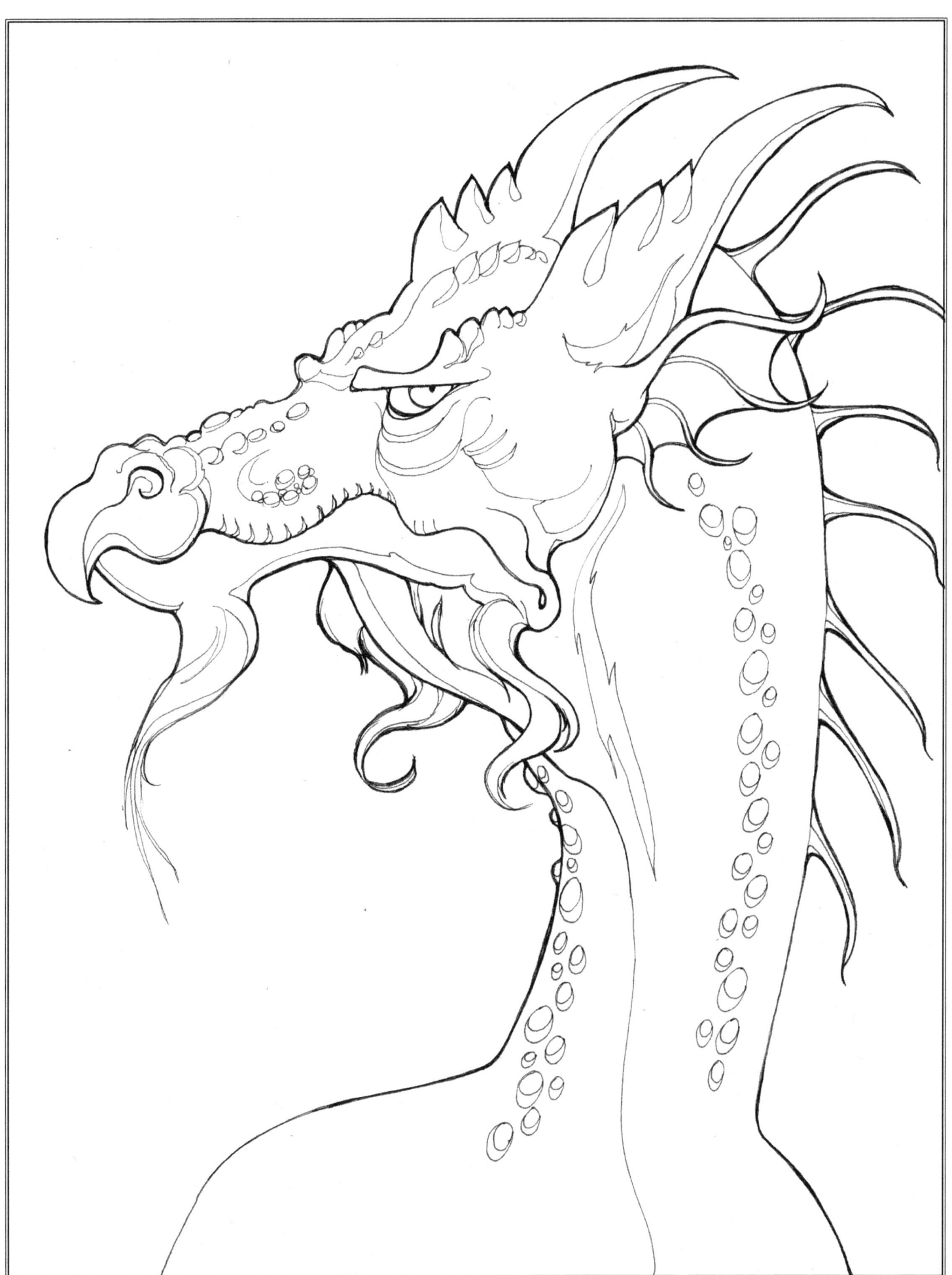

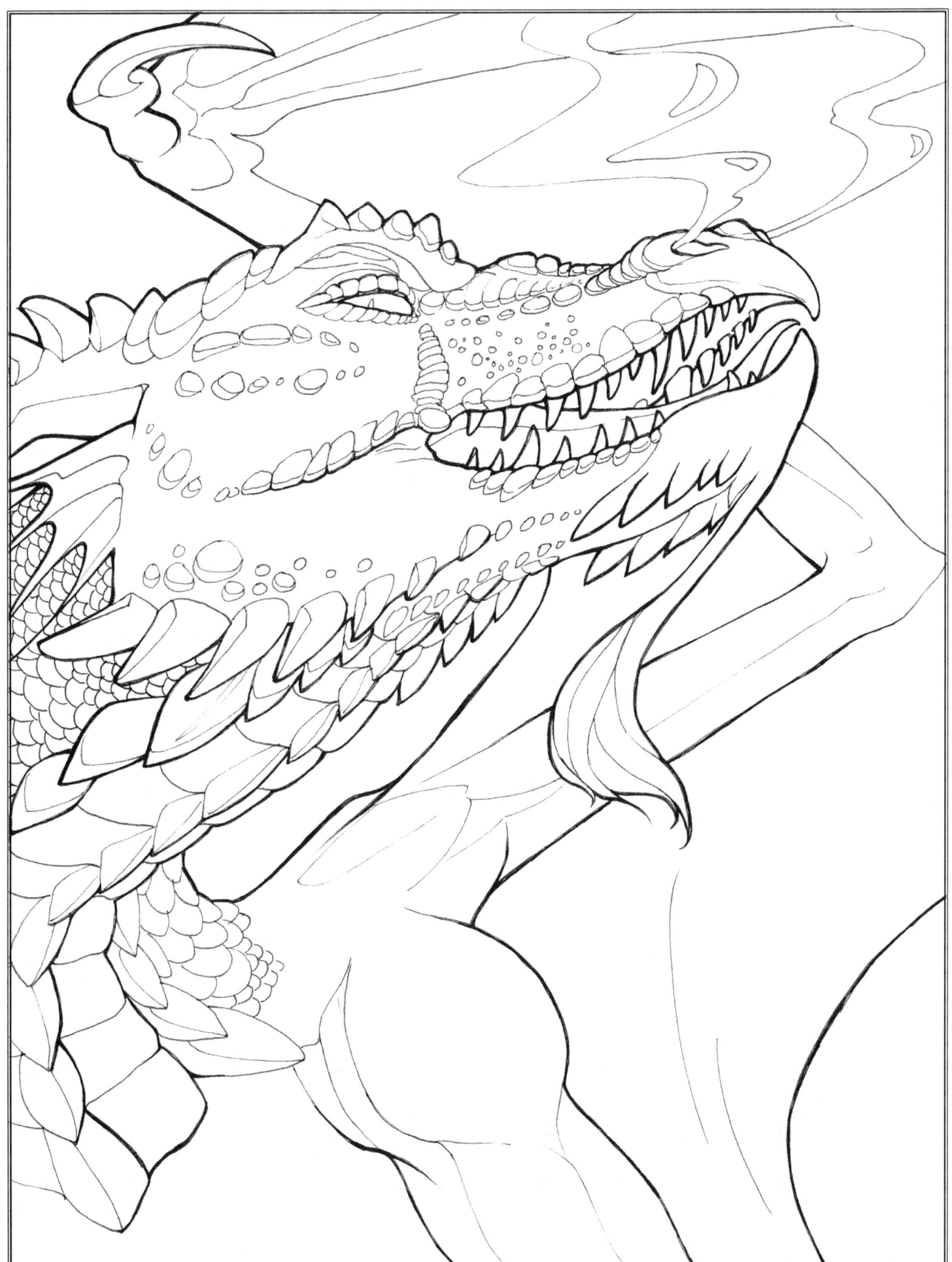

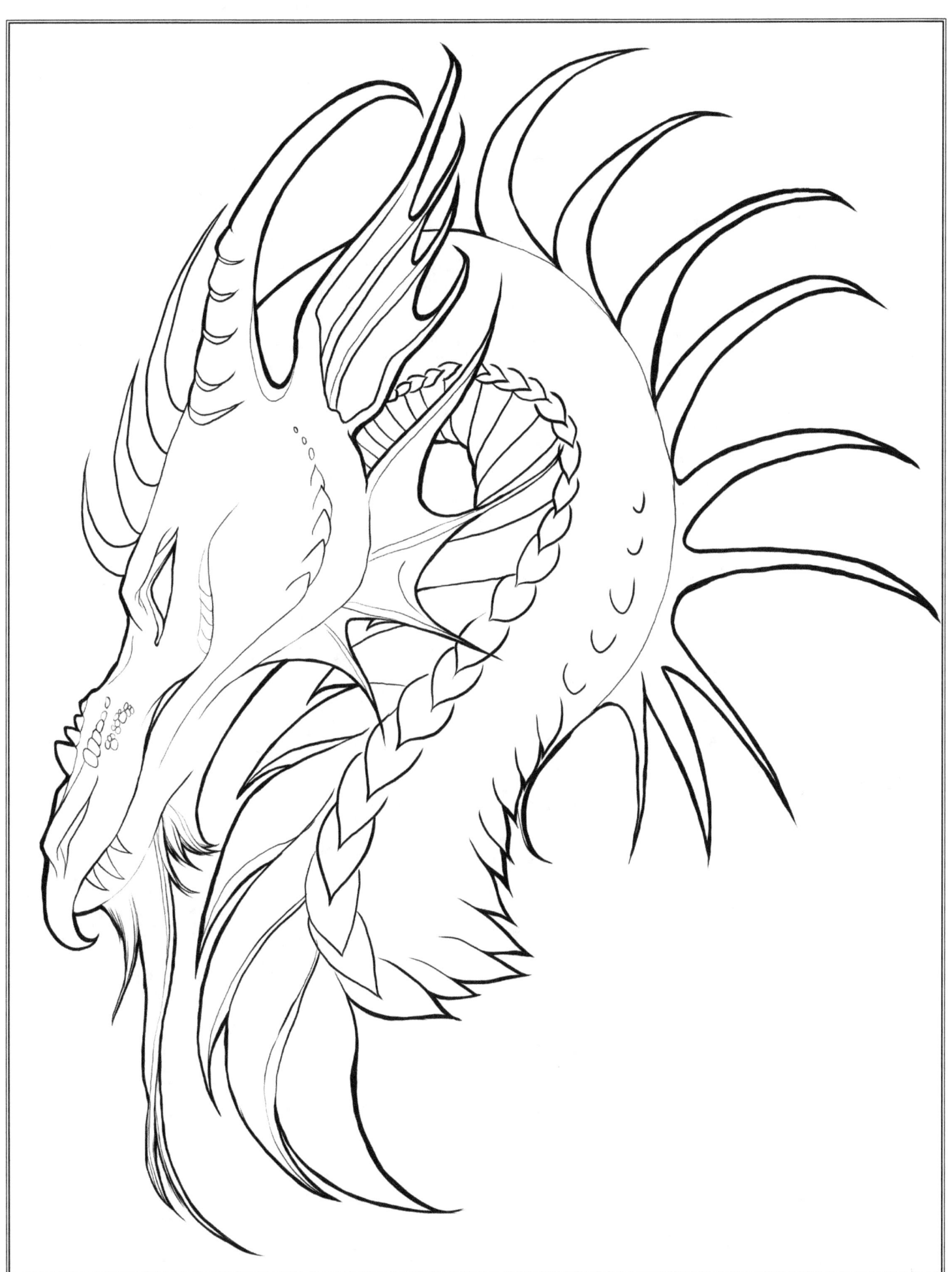

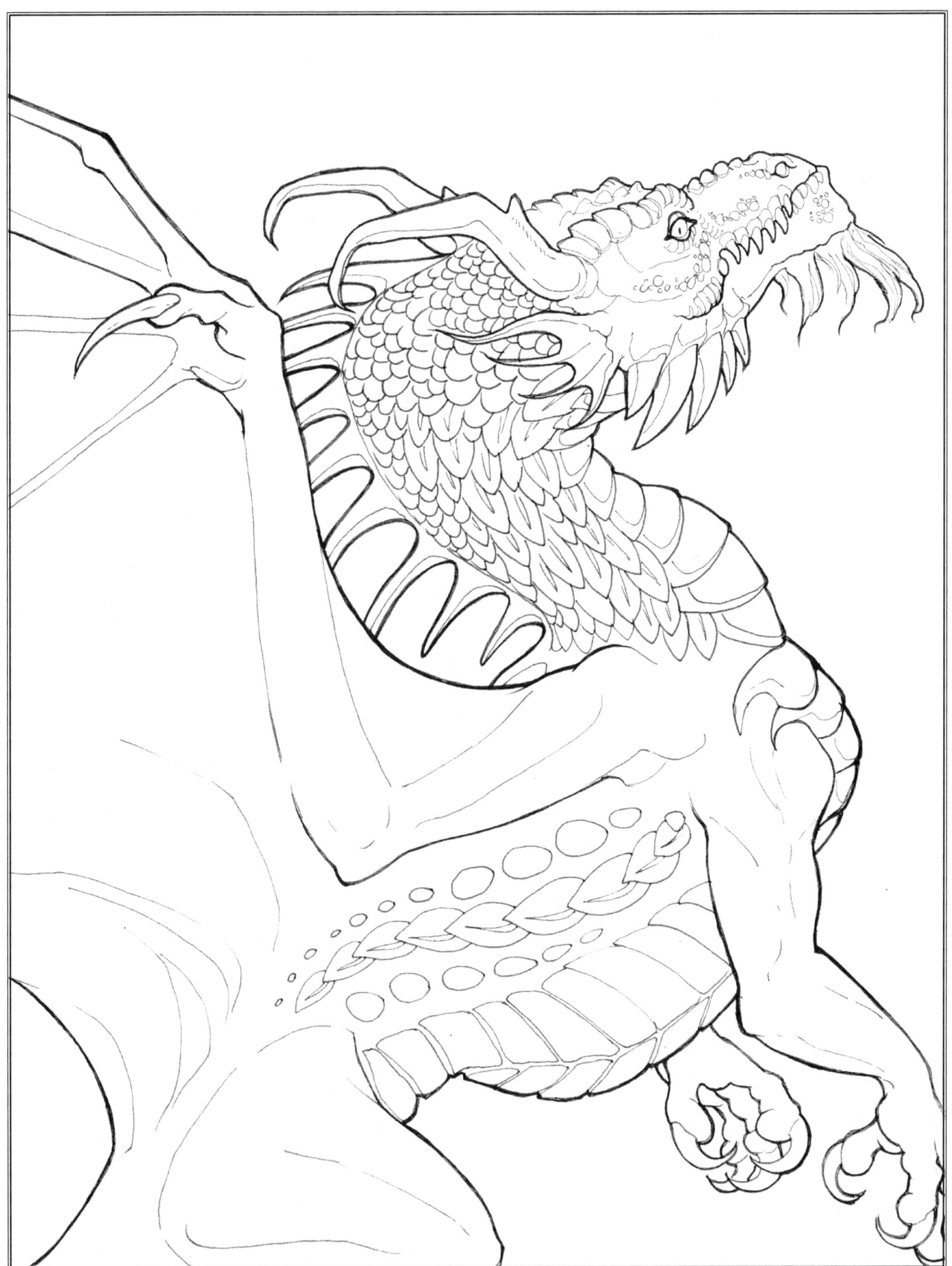

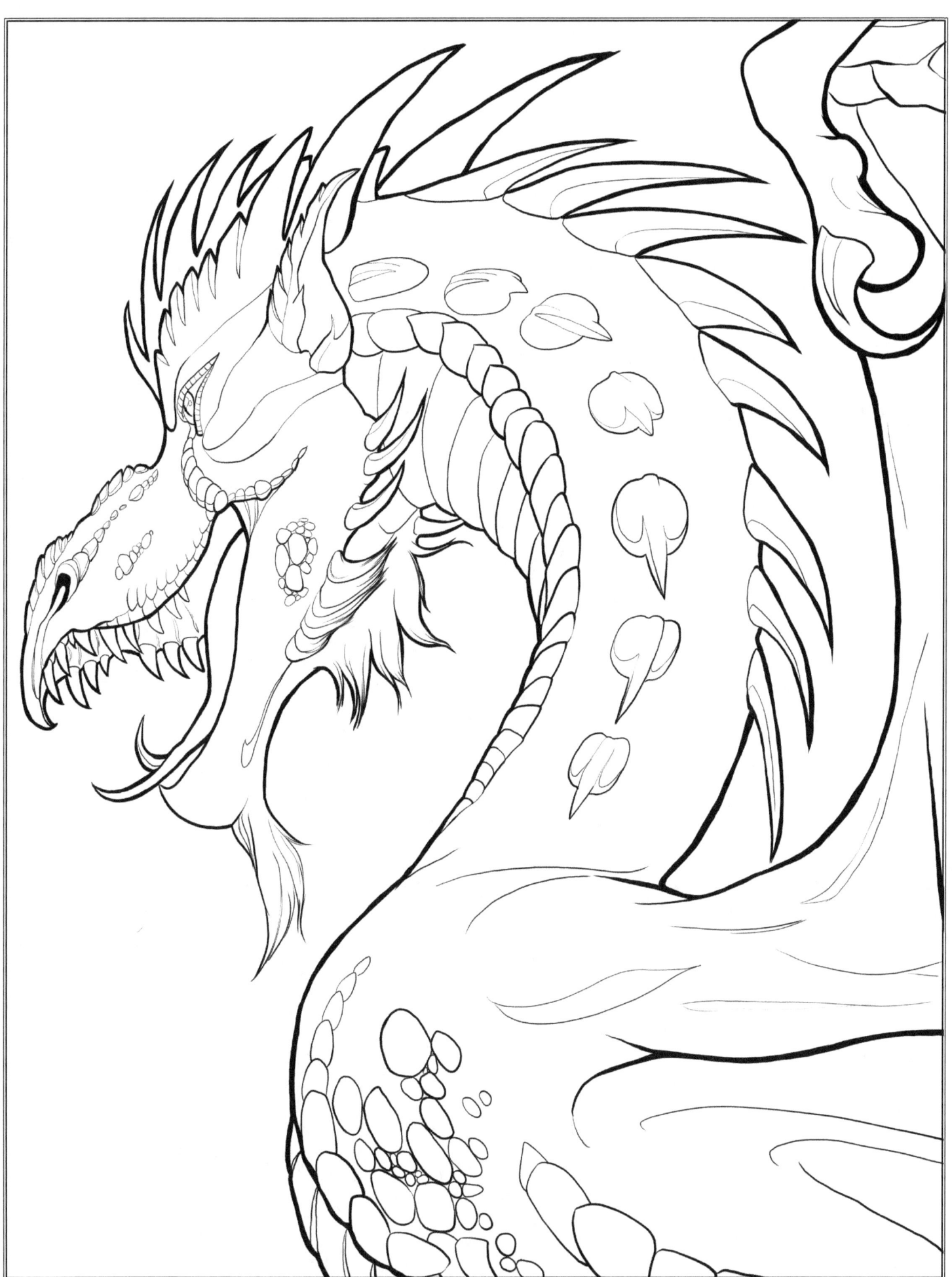

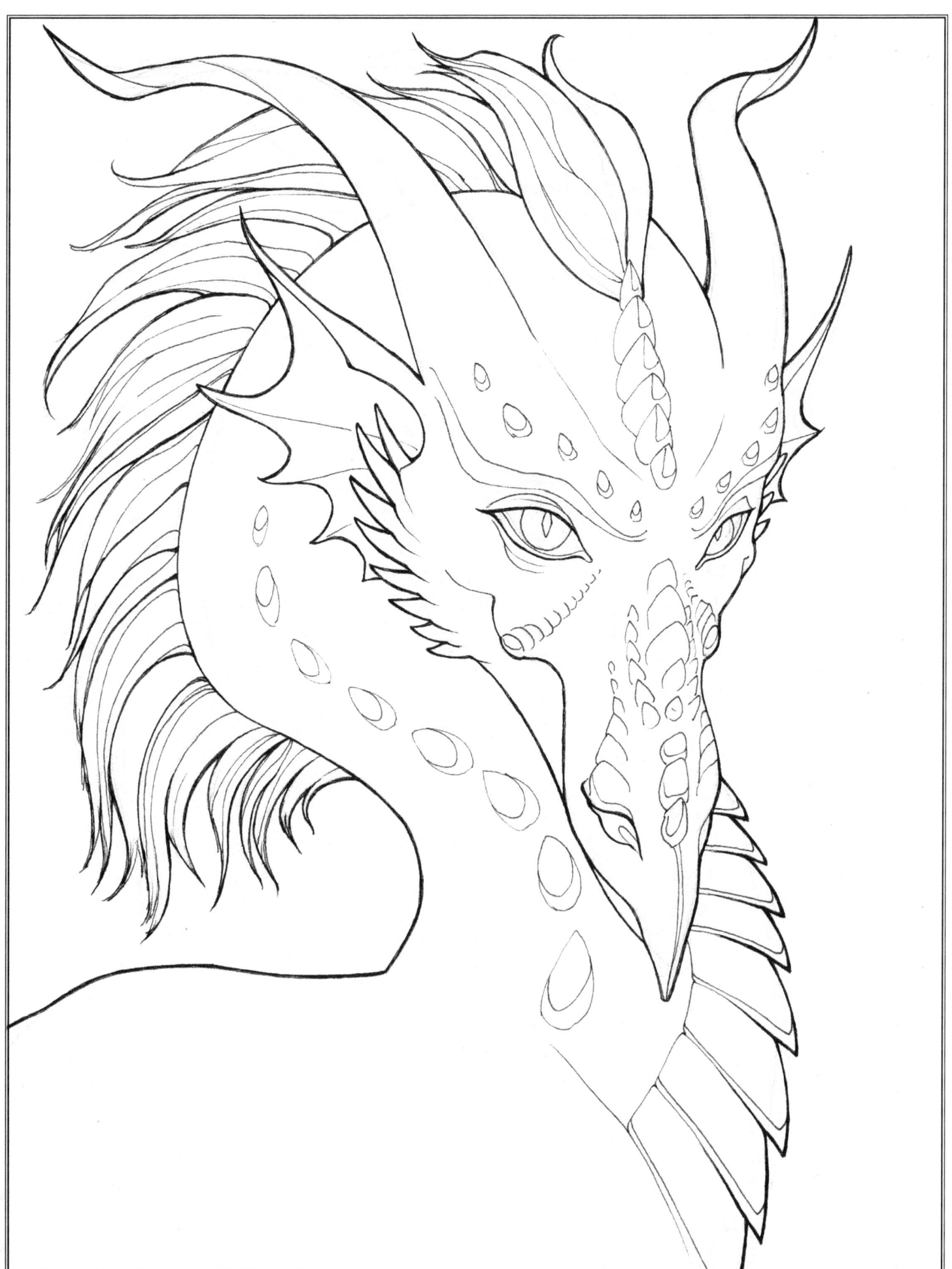

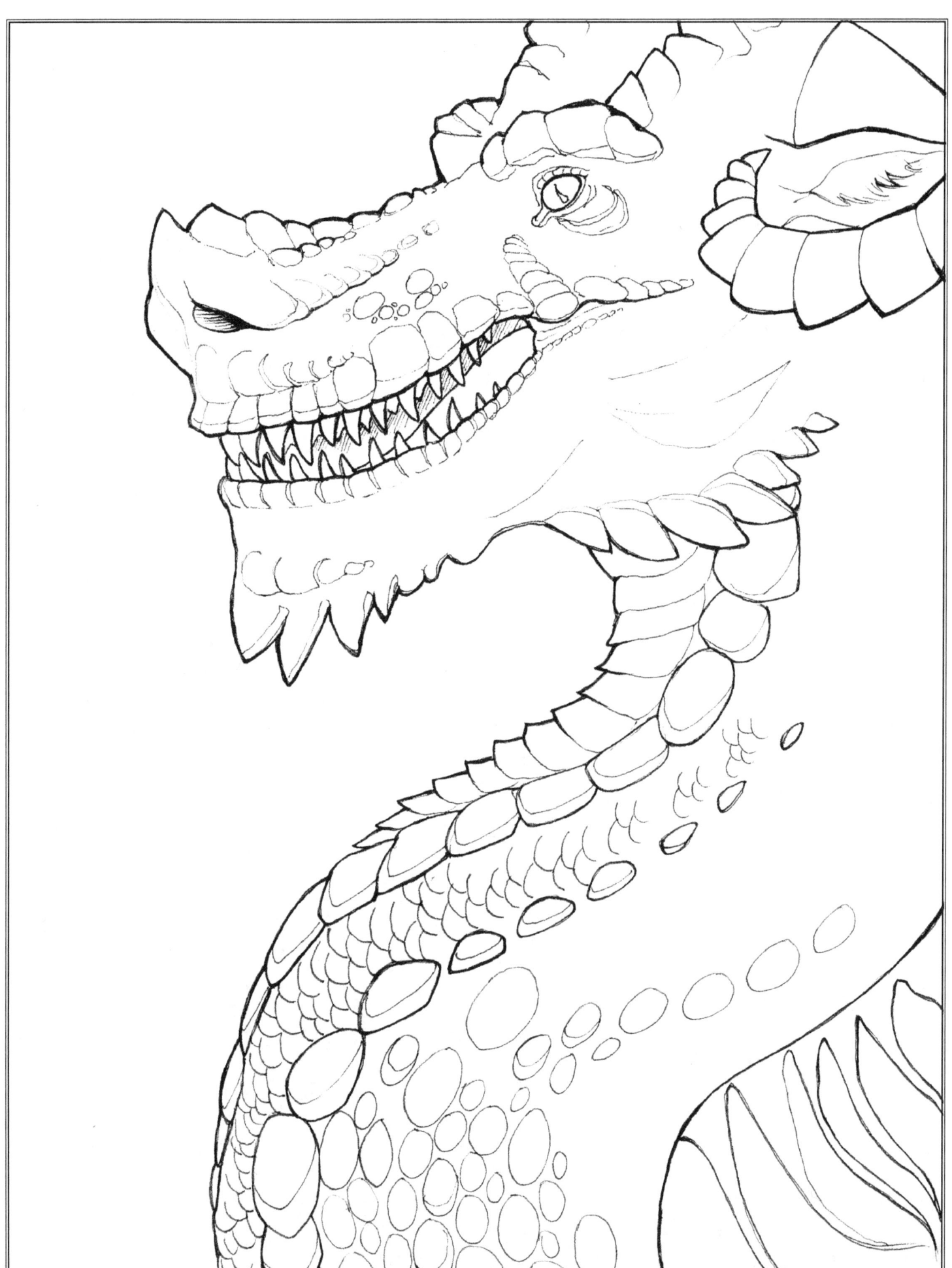

www.ingramcontent.com/pod-product-compliance
Lightning Source LLC
Chambersburg PA
CBHW060007230526
45472CB00008B/1980

* 9 7 8 1 9 7 9 9 7 3 7 7 9 *